EXPLORERS AND COLONIZATION™

LEWIS AND CLARK

Famed Explorers of the American Frontier

JENNIFER SWANSON

ROSEN
PUBLISHING®

New York

Published in 2017 by The Rosen Publishing Group, Inc.
29 East 21st Street, New York, NY 10010

First Edition

Library of Congress Cataloging in Publication Data

Names: Swanson, Jennifer, author.
Title: Lewis and Clark: Famed Explorers of the American Frontier / Jennifer Swanson.
Description: First edition. | New York : Rosen Publishing, 2017 | Series:
Spotlight on explorers and colonization | Includes bibliographical
references and index.
Identifiers: LCCN 2016018989| ISBN 9781508172406 (library bound) | ISBN
9781508172376 (pbk.) | ISBN 9781508172383 (6-pack)
Subjects: LCSH: Lewis and Clark Expedition (1804–1806)—Juvenile literature.
| West (U.S.)—Discovery and exploration—Juvenile literature. | West
(U.S.) —Description and travel—Juvenile literature. | Lewis, Meriwether,
1774-1809—Juvenile literature. | Clark, William, 1770–1838—Juvenile
literature. | Explorers—West (U.S.) —Biography—Juvenile literature.
Classification: LCC F592.7 .S92 2016 | DDC 917.804/2—dc23
LC record available at https://lccn.loc.gov/2016018989

Manufactured in China

CONTENTS

MEET LEWIS AND CLARK

Meriwether Lewis and William Clark are two of the most famous explorers of North America. They are responsible for mapping more than 3,700 miles (6,000 kilometers) of unfamiliar terrain. On their trek to discover a navigable route to the Pacific Ocean, they met many new people and saw sights that had been unknown to Americans before. These sights included over forty-five tribes of Native Americans and three hundred new species of animals. They also visited the most massive mountains in North America. It was the greatest wilderness trip ever!

The United States and France struck a deal in 1803 for the purchase of 828,000 square miles (2,145,000 square kilometers) of uncharted land to the west of the Mississippi River.

President Thomas Jefferson had always dreamed of expanding the United States into the western territories. At the beginning of 1803, his dream was realized. He began talks with France to acquire a large tract of land that was at that time known as Louisiana. It stretched 828,000 square miles (2,145,000 square kilometers) west of the Mississippi River. This $15 million land deal became known as the Louisiana Purchase.

Jefferson was so anxious to learn more about the western country that he couldn't even wait until the contract was complete to begin exploring. In January 1803, President Jefferson sent a secret letter to the US Congress asking for $2,500 to fund an expedition. His request was granted. The Louisiana Purchase was signed in May 1803. After that, Jefferson sent Meriwether Lewis and William Clark on their famous journey to explore the West.

Meriwether Lewis was a family friend of Thomas Jefferson's. He eventually became the third president's private secretary and assistant. William Clark was born to the son of a plantation farmer. He joined the regular army as an officer. In the army, he met Meriwether Lewis. They were both trained to live in the wilderness and loved adventure! When Lewis contacted his old friend Clark and asked him to join in the expedition, Clark agreed eagerly.

BEFORE LEWIS AND CLARK

Lewis and Clark were not the first explorers to head west on the North American continent. They followed such men as Coronado, de Soto, Chouteau, and La Salle. These men had spoken of encounters with Native Americans who lived and roamed across the western country. But none of these explorers were Americans. The newly elected president set out to fix that.

President Jefferson had begun petitioning for a westward expedition long before 1803. His father was a founding member of the Loyalty Company. This company gave out grants of land west of the Allegheny River.

William Clark created all of the maps from the Lewis and Clark expedition and helped to decide which routes to take to get to the Pacific Ocean.

Meriwether Lewis's grand-father was also a member. Jefferson encouraged the United States government to explore and map the western territory. He had several goals for Lewis and Clark's mission. They were to meet and establish trade with the Native Americans, conduct scientific observations, and find a passable route to the Pacific Ocean from the east.

THE CORPS OF DISCOVERY

Setting out on an expedition like this required a huge amount of planning. President Jefferson wanted to make sure that Lewis and Clark were able to handle any situation that they encountered. So he sent Lewis to Philadelphia for training. There he learned about mapmaking and surveying, plants, fossils, and even medicine. The men who taught Lewis were all members of the American Philosophical Society, a group formed by Benjamin Franklin in order to increase the knowledge of science. The society, at Jefferson's request, helped to fund a part of the expedition.

Thomas Jefferson was fascinated by the west. Even before the Louisiana Purchase was complete, he had made plans to send explorers out to find the Pacific Ocean.

While in Philadelphia, Lewis gathered supplies for the mission. He obtained guns, ammunition, food, clothing, medical supplies, and camping equipment. It turned out to be an enormous haul!

Lewis and Clark recruited members for the newly formed Corps of Discovery, as they called themselves. Since both Lewis and Clark were former soldiers, it only made sense that they invited twenty-seven soldiers to join them on their expedition.

Lewis and Clark made much of the journey in their keelboat. It had both sails and oars so they could use it when there was no wind.

The Corps also included a few civilians, or non-military people. Three of these were Toussaint Charbonneau, the guide; George Drouillard, a fur trader; and York,

Ed. Velell

Clark's slave. Eventually this group included Sacagawea, a female Shoshone Indian and wife of Charbonneau. Sacagawea's son also came along. Overall, the Corps of Discovery was a diverse group made up of thirty-one men, one woman, and a baby.

At last the time came. The expedition was outfitted with supplies, food, and clothing. Lewis and Clark were trained. They had also learned codes so that their communications with President Jefferson could not be intercepted and read.

The Corps set out on May 21, 1804, from St. Louis, Missouri. They rode on a 55-foot (17-meter) shallow boat that carried almost twelve tons of supplies. The crew used oars and poles to propel themselves 2,000 miles (3,200 kilometers) upriver.

HISTORIC INTRODUCTIONS

The expedition's first encounter with Native Americans occurred near Council Bluff, Iowa, on August 2, 1803. This friendly gathering was the first time representatives of the United States government and the Oto tribe met formally. The Oto were Sioux natives who were related to both the Iowa and Missouri tribes.

Lewis used the diplomacy tools that he had learned while studying in Philadelphia. He understood that gift giving and trade were important to Native Americans. The Corps dressed in their finest and paraded into the council. They displayed their

Meriwether Lewis and William Clark held the first of many meetings with local Native American tribes at Council Bluff to introduce themselves as representatives of the United States.

weapons, a sign of strength and respect, and gave gifts to the chiefs. Unfortunately, the chiefs they picked to receive the gifts were not of the highest rank. The Oto were not pleased with this oversight. Overall, though, the meeting went well and set the pattern for future councils with Native Americans. One result of this first meeting was that a delegation of Indian chiefs went to meet with President Jefferson.

THE TETON SIOUX

Lewis and Clark were somewhat nervous to meet the Teton Sioux. They had been warned that the Teton Sioux might confront them. The meeting went on for three days. Several near-fights took place. The natives were unhappy to have the expedition moving through their territory. They controlled the trade on both sides of the Missouri River through South Dakota.

As the Corps prepared to head upriver, a large crowd of armed Teton Sioux approached them. They demanded tobacco as a toll to pass on the river. The members of the Corps drew their own guns, ready to fire

Lewis and Clark sometimes used a canoe to travel up the river, which meant they were very close to the shore and the Native Americans who lived there.

if necessary. Would their expedition end in a hail of bullets? At the last moment, though, the Corps handed over some tobacco. The Teton Sioux then allowed them to pass peacefully. Clark, however, was angry at the way they had been treated. He ignored the tribe completely on the return trip.

FINDING AN UNLIKELY INTERPRETER

In November 1804, the Corps began looking for a place to set their winter camp. Lewis and Clark knew that travel through the northwest would be too dangerous during the cold winter months. So they built a fort on the banks of the Missouri River in North Dakota. They called it Fort Mandan after the Mandan tribe that lived across the river. Lewis and Clark enjoyed the friendly Mandans and their fellow tribes, such as the Hidatsa. The Corps traded food and other goods with them. These tribes were allied against the Sioux. The added protection of over 1,400 armed Native

Sacagawea was a great choice to help the explorers because she knew not just the language, but also the land they were attempting to cross.

Americans was also welcomed by Lewis and Clark.

They spent the frigid winter inside the fort for the most part, except for hunts to bring back food. Lewis and Clark knew that they needed an interpreter who could speak to the different native tribes. A French Canadian fur trader by the name of Toussaint Charbonneau applied for the job.

While Lewis and Clark were not exactly thrilled with Charbonneau, they saw the value that his seventeen-year-old Shoshone bride, Sacagawea, provided. Sacagawea could not understand English, but she could speak both Shoshone and Hidatsa. Charbonneau spoke both Hidatsa and French, so the two would work together as interpreters.

In March 1804, less than one month after giving birth to her son, Jean-Baptiste, Sacagawea joined the expedition to head west. It was unusual to bring a woman, much less her infant child, on this multiyear trek. And yet, Sacagawea was a useful member of the Corps. She not only translated, but the tribes noticed the fact that she was traveling with white men. Sacagawea's presence with the Corps made the tribes more open to speaking with them. That meant the Corps had less open confrontations with the Native American tribes they met along the way.

LIFE ON THE TRAIL

Once the members of the expedition left the safety of the Mandan tribe, they headed into a part of the West where they encountered a large amount of wildlife: elk, deer, goats, buffalos, and grizzly bears. The group wrote the very first scientific descriptions of the grizzly bears and their habitats. On June 15, 1805, Lewis was hunting by himself. He shot a buffalo. Suddenly a grizzly bear rushed toward him! He tried to shoot his gun, but he had not reloaded it. Lewis ran into

Lewis and Clark had many encounters with new and dangerous animals on their expedition, some of which they had never encountered east of the Mississippi River.

a nearby river. Luckily, the bear did not follow him there.

The rough terrain and extreme climate took their toll on the members of the expedition. Life on the trail meant that they were always on the alert for animals and Native Americans.

Lewis and Clark never lost their focus. Every day, they recorded the distances they had traveled. They made maps of the country for future travelers.

THE GREAT FALLS

Whenever they could, the Corps traveled by river. Not only was it easier than walking, but they could cover great distances much more quickly. However, traveling by river could also be dangerous. Rapids sometimes capsized the pirogues, or small boats, and canoes. Quick thinking by Sacagawea during one event prevented them from losing valuable maps and charts. Still, following the rivers was the fastest route west, so Lewis and Clark paddled on.

On June 3, 1805, the expedition reached an important crossroad, a fork in the

Lewis and Clark wanted Sacagawea to come along on the voyage for skills as an interpreter, but she proved to be a valuable member of the Corps for other reasons, too.

Missouri River. Should they go north or south? Only one branch would take them to the Rocky Mountains. According to the Indians at Fort Mandan, if they found the Great Falls, it would point them in the correct direction.

After some debate, Lewis and Clark decided that the south fork was most likely the correct branch of the river. To be sure, Lewis went forward on foot with a small number of men. They moved ahead quickly.

Lewis and Clark created maps of the rivers they crossed, making sure to mark the major lakes and the Great Falls on their drawings.

When Lewis's group found the falls, they would report back to the rest of the Corps. After four days of travel, Lewis was overjoyed to hear the roaring of the

Great Falls. They had chosen the correct river!

The excitement did not last long. The Great Falls were huge and the rapids were extremely dangerous. This made crossing them impossible. Instead, the party had to build temporary wagons to portage the canoes and supplies across them to get to a navigable stretch of the river. It was hard, exhausting work to haul the heavy supplies around the 21-mile (34-km) long falls. The heat was unbearable and the men had to stop frequently to rest. It took the Corps more than one month to reach a point in the Missouri River where they could use their canoes again.

A WAY OVER
THE MOUNTAINS

Lewis and Clark knew they needed horses to go over the Rockies. The Native Americans at Fort Mandan advised them to seek out the Shoshone tribe. The Shoshone chief they met happened to be Sacagawea's brother! He allowed her to negotiate for the horses. The price, though, grew every day. The first day, Lewis and Clark paid a knife and a shirt for a horse. The next day it cost more. Eventually, it cost one-hundred rounds of ammunition for a single horse. The Corps had no choice but to pay it. Without the horses, they would not make it to the Pacific Ocean on the other side of

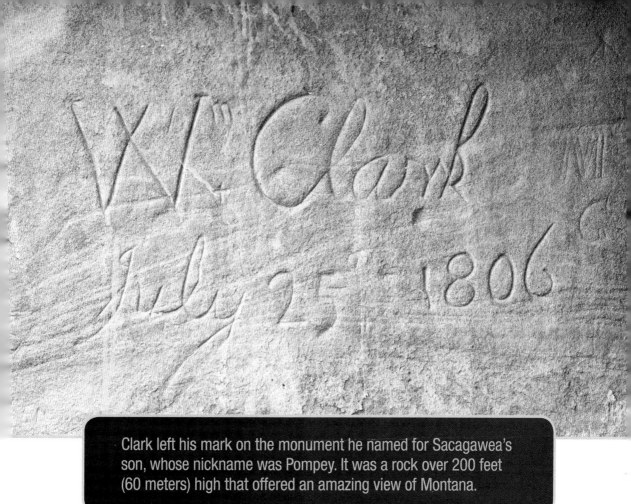

Clark left his mark on the monument he named for Sacagawea's son, whose nickname was Pompey. It was a rock over 200 feet (60 meters) high that offered an amazing view of Montana.

the country. Aside from the horses, Lewis and Clark also got details about an old path through the Rockies, one used by the Nez Perce tribe. If they hadn't learned about the trail and traded for the horses, they might never have made it over the mountains.

DEADLY DIVIDE: THE BITTERROOTS

The most dangerous part of their crossing was following a path through the Bitterroot Mountains. Even though the Corps had the help of a Shoshone guide named "Old Tony," they still got lost. They endured freezing temperatures, rain, and snow as they traveled over 9 miles (14 km) of steep mountains. Many of the trees in the area had fallen, leaving logs spread across the land like a giant obstacle course. This meant that both the men and their horses had to expend extra effort to climb over them or go around them. During the

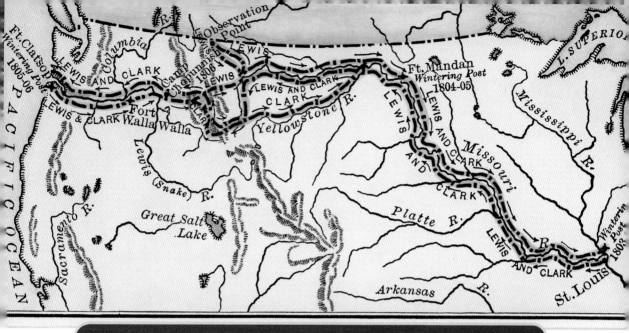

The trip out west was hazardous and the expedition sometimes had to find different ways to get around areas that were too difficult to climb.

trek, they climbed a peak 7,000 feet (2,100 meters) high.

Food was scarce. The men grew so hungry that they ate three of the horses to stay alive. After eleven long days, the members were on the verge of starvation. Finally, they emerged on the other side. The Nez Perce Indians greeted the relieved Corps members with nuts and fruit.

OCEAN!

After fifteen long months, the Corps finally reached their destination: the Pacific Ocean. There, Lewis and Clark hoped to find a trading ship to take them back home. Instead, the weary travelers met never-ending rain, high winds, and rough seas. They had no choice but to retreat to a safer place inland. They built a camp there called Station Camp. For ten days, they stayed there hunting, fishing, and regaining their strength after the tough mountain trek.

The Chinook and Clatsop Native American tribes visited them. These tribes traded regularly with ships that came past.

Fort Clatsop is still in place today. Although it doesn't look like much, it was home to the expedition for an entire winter.

Unfortunately for Lewis and Clark, the one time a ship stopped by, the tribes did not tell them about it. Reluctantly, the expedition voted to spend the winter inland, near Oregon. They built Fort Clatsop in this area. In March 1806, they headed home, via a land route.

HEADED HOME

The return route was no easier than the trip out had been. On the way home, the Corps travelled against river currents, experienced long portages, and skirmished with hostile Native Americans.

The Nez Perce welcomed the Corps, but the Blackfoot tribe was not as friendly. After Lewis and Clark had separated to explore the area, Lewis came upon the Blackfoot tribe. The two groups camped together. But during the night, a fight broke out and two natives were killed. Lewis and his men left quickly to avoid the same fate.

Reunited at the Missouri River, Lewis and Clark pushed their men to get home. They covered 60 to 80 miles (95 to 130 km) a day, a huge feat at the time. Along the

way, they were met with surprise by other adventurers. The Corps of Discovery had been gone so long that they had been given up for dead.

Charbonneau, Sacagawea, and their son (now almost two years old), left the group to stay in North Dakota in August 1806. The rest of the Corps continued on.

Lewis and Clark were anxious to avoid another confrontation in Teton Sioux territory. As a result, they kept their canoes in the middle of the river. They ignored the armed, grim-faced warriors lining both banks of the river.

HEROES ARRIVE

On September 23, 1806, two years and four months after had they set out, Lewis and Clark entered St. Louis, Missouri. They were hailed as heroes. Their expedition had been a huge success! Not only had they mapped a trail out west, but they also brought back information on plants, animals, and the terrain. Most important, Lewis and Clark had established contact with more than forty-five different Native American tribes. Many of these tribes would go on to set up talks with the United States government.

A surprising outcome was that only one person died on the entire two-year trip,

PHILADELPHIA November 10.

More Wonders.—The following extract of a letter is copied from the National Intelligencer. The Rocky mountain sheep beats the horned frog *all hollow*.

U. S. Gaz.

Extract of a letter from a gentleman at St. Charles, to a gentleman in this town, dated 23d September, 1806.

I have the pleasure to inform you of the arrival of captains Lewis and Clark. They were the first white people that ever visited that country. By the best accounts they could get, there are about ninety or one hundred thousand inhabitants, (Indians) on the west side of the Rocky Mountains: horses without number. It is thought to be a very poor Indian that did not own 300 horses. Not an iron tool among them. They erected a fort on the sea shore, and engraved their names. They have brought a number of curiosities; among which is a wild sheep; its head and horns weigh about 80 or 90 pounds. He was caught on the Rocky

Sergeant Floyd, because of appendicitis. President Jefferson was extremely happy to hear of their safe return. He hailed the entire Corps as heroes to the US Congress. They had performed "heroic and patriotic deeds" that reflected well on their country, he said.

LEGACY AND HONORS

Every member of the Corps of Discovery was seen as a hero and a great contributor to the wealth of information gained by the United States. Collectively, they mapped huge portions of the West, identified hundreds of plants and animals, and created new opportunities for trade and contact with Native Americans.

The journals compiled by Lewis and Clark serve as the first and most complete view of the Native American tribes who lived at that time. No other such records exist. While Lewis and Clark did not forge friendships with every tribe they encountered, they were some of the

Lewis and Clark depended heavily on the help of Sacagawea and her husband, not just as interpreters, but also because they knew the land and the people.

first white men to meet and converse with them. The fact that they were successful in working with a few of the tribes is especially important. Without the help of many of the Native American tribes, the mission would not have succeeded.

Long-term, the Corps created great change. Right after their return, from 1806 to 1812, the fur trade increased. Lewis and Clark did not find the Northwest Passage they sought. Neither did they start the fur trade or create a huge influx of westward settlement. Still, they influenced both of these later movements. Most important was the wealth of scientific data they noted. In a very real sense, their expedition opened up the way to the West.

The effects on the native peoples were devastating, though. The increased contact with fur traders, soldiers, and missionaries spread smallpox. The worst epidemic occurred in 1837 and all but wiped out the Mandan tribes.

Over time, the way of life of the Native Americans changed completely. They were shuffled onto reservations and forced into schools that ignored their traditions. Disease thinned their numbers. Despite these hardships, though, they survived to become valued members of American society.

Many monuments and memorials commemorate Lewis and Clark's famous trek, one of the greatest expeditions ever completed within the United States.

GLOSSARY

ammunition Any material, means, weapons, or other objects used in conflict.

appendicitis An inflammation of the appendix that if not treated can cause it to burst, leading to death.

Bitterroots These mountains, part of the larger Rocky Mountain range, form part of the border between today's states of Idaho and Montana.

diplomacy The art of conducting negotiations.

expedition An excursion, journey, or voyage made for some specific purpose, as of war or exploration.

focus To concentrate.

frigid Extremely cold.

Louisiana Purchase The purchase of the western half of the Mississippi River basin in 1803 from France by the United States.

navigable Deep and wide enough to provide passage to boats or ships.

negotiate To deal or bargain with another or others, as in the preparation of a treaty or contract.

petition A formal request for a favor that is addressed to a person in authority or power.

pirogue A native boat, especially an American dugout.

portage The carrying of boats, goods, and other items overland from one navigable waterway to another.

terrain A tract of land, especially its natural features.

The Journals of the Lewis and Clark Expedition
The University of Nebraska-Lincoln
1400 R Street
Lincoln, NE 68588
(402) 472-7211
Website: http://lewisandclarkjournals.unl.edu
This website has the text of the Nebraska edition of the
    Lewis and Clark journals, edited by Gary E. Moulton.

Lewis and Clark Expedition
National Park Service
Website: https://www.nps.gov/nr/travel/lewisandclark
    /jef.htm
This register of historic places is run by the National Park
    Service. It includes a travel itinerary and list of sites
    from Virginia to Oregon that commemorate the Lewis
    and Clark journey.

Lewis and Clark Fort Mandan Foundation
Intersection of US Hwy 83 and ND Hwy 200A
Washburn, ND 58577
(701) 462-8535
Website: http://www.fortmandan.com/plan/lewis-and
    -clark-interpretive-center
The Lewis and Clark Fort Mandan Foundation works to
    preserve knowledge about the people, places, and
    land of the area and the Missouri River.

Lewis and Clark National Historic Trail Interpretive Center
4201 Giant Springs Road
Great Falls, MT 59405
(406) 727-8733
Website: http://www.visitmt.com/listings/general/
    museum/lewis-and-clark-national-historic-trail-
    interpretive-center.html
This center includes exhibits and ranger programs that
    highlight Lewis and Clark's journey through Montana.

National Archives Museum
Constitution Avenue NW
Washington, DC 20408
(866) 272-6272
Website: https://www.archives.gov/education/lessons
    /lewis-clark
Here, you can take a look at the documents associated
    with the Lewis and Clark expedition.

Websites

Because of the changing nature of internet links, Rosen
Publishing has developed an online list of websites
related to the subject of this book. This site is updated
regularly. Please use this link to access the list:

http://www.rosenlinks.com/SEC/lc

Domnauer, Teresa. *The Lewis & Clark Expedition*. New York, NY: Children's Press, 2013.

Gunderson, Jessica, and Colleen M. Madden. *Your Life as a Private on the Lewis and Clark Expedition*. North Mankato, MN: Picture Window, 2013.

Jazynka, Kitson. *Sacagawea*. Washington, DC: National Geographic Adventures Classic, 2013.

Jeffrey, Gary. *The Explorations of Lewis and Clark*. New York, NY: Gareth Stevens, 2012.

Keller, Susanna. *The True Story of Lewis and Clark*. New York, NY: PowerKids Press, 2013.

Levy, Janey. *Lewis and Clark in Their Own Words*. New York, NY: Gareth Stevens, 2014.

Morley, Jacqueline, Mark Bergin, and David Salariya. *You Wouldn't Want to Explore with Lewis and Clark! An Epic Journey You'd Rather Not Make*. New York, NY: Children's/Scholastic, 2013.

Stille, Darlene R. *The Journals of Lewis and Clark*. Chicago, IL: Heinemann Library, 2013.

BIBLIOGRAPHY

Brandt, Anthony. *The Journals of Lewis and Clark.* Washington, DC: National Geographic Adventures Classic, 2002.

Christian, Shirley. *Before Lewis and Clark: The Story of the Chouteaus, the French Dynasty That Ruled America's Frontier.* New York, NY: Farrar, Straus and Giroux, 2004.

Gilman, Carolyn. *Lewis and Clark: Across the Divide.* Washington, DC: Smithsonian, 2004.

Huser, Verne. *On the River with Lewis and Clark.* College Station, TX: Texas A & M University Press, 2004.

Lewis, Meriwether, William Clark, and Gary E. Moulton. *The Lewis and Clark Journals: An American Epic of Discovery.* Lincoln, NE: University of Nebraska Press, 2003.

Library of Congress. "Meriwether Lewis & William Clark - Meet Amazing Americans | America's Library - Library of Congress." 2000. http://www.americaslibrary.gov/aa/lewisandclark/aa_lewisandclark_subj.html.

Morris, Larry E. *The Fate of the Corps: What Became of the Lewis and Clark Explorers After the Expedition.* New Haven, CT: Yale University Press, 2004.

National Park Service. "Lewis & Clark National Historic Trail." Retrieved February 26, 2016. https://www.nps.gov/nr/travel/lewisandclark/jef.htm.

INDEX

About the Author

Jennifer Swanson is the author of more than twenty-five non-fiction books for children. She got her love of history from her mother, who not only spent many hours reading about the explorers but took her children to the places of their expeditions. Swanson has visited the sites of Marquette's and Joliet's landing in Green Bay, Wisconsin, as well as the Gateway Arch in St. Louis, the spot where Lewis and Clark left on their journey.

Photo Credits